AROUND THE HOUSE

AROUND THE HOUSE

David Frazier

Series Editor: Herbert Wise

quick fox

New York · London · Tokyo

International Standard Book Number: 0-8256-3143-2
Library of Congress Catalog Card Number: 78-70994

Printed in Japan.

No part of this book may be reproduced or transmitted in any
form or by any means, electronic or mechanical, including
photocopying, without permission in writing from the publisher:
Quick Fox, A Division of Music Sales Corporation, 33 West 60th Street,
New York 10023.

In Great Britain: Book Sales Ltd., 78 Newman Street, London W1P 3LA.

In Canada: Gage Trade Publishing, P.O. Box 5000, 164 Commander Blvd.,
          Agincourt, Ontario M1S 3C7.

In Japan: Quick Fox, 4-26-22 Jingumae, Shibuya-ku, Tokyo 150.

In Australia: Quick Fox, 27 Clarendon Street, Artarmon, Sydney
          NSW 2064.

In Germany: Music Sales Gmbh, Kölner Strasse 199, D-5000 Cologne 90
          West Germany.

Design: Iris Weinstein
Landscape Consultant: Timothy DuVal, Plant Specialists, Inc., New York
Locations: Jamie Simpson
Architectural symbols: Rick Rakusin
Flagging patterns and construction: Building Stone Institute, New York

AROUND THE HOUSE

As with the other books in this series, AROUND
THE HOUSE gives us a view into other people's
houses. AROUND THE HOUSE is a book about
landscaping and, while it might be audacious to
try to improve on nature, it is important to view
landscaping in its proper perspective.

Landscaping is the opposite of natural, rolling
hills—it is the art of containment. It is ornamental, yet underlying the decorative aspect is a
comfortable sense of spaciousness that often is
more psychological than real. Landscaping is
thought of as the quintessential formal art, but
many of the photographs have the delightful
feeling of casualness. It is a curious art, intensely
personal. And the people whose works are
shown on these pages share an aesthetic that
demands expression not with paints and canvas,
not with clay and wire or pen and ink but with
the careful rearranging of a pinpoint of nature
into a new, harmonically pleasing whole.

If the art seems impenetrable, happily one is
guided by the materials and limitations of
geography. Travel across the country, as I did,
and the raw materials of nature—the trees and
shrubs, the soil and stone—along with the brush-
strokes of civilization—fences, pools, stone steps,
patios, bridges—dramatically change. Planting
cactus in Minneapolis or building a hot house in
Arizona are automatically ruled out, for so
sensitive an art is equally practical. The object,

then, is to create a panorama of natural beauty that in turn imparts a sense of privacy, of security, of spaciousness, or serenity, that directly affects the homeowner's psychological state.

One of my first thoughts in organizing this book was to visit the most opulent homes I could locate. I associated opulence with expanse and both with landscape excellence. But as you wander through the pages of this book you will discover just as many photographs of perfectly ordinary objects and scenes that bespeak any- thing but wealth, yet are ingeniously conceived. Stone steps descending into secluded glades. Gazebos as gossamer as the finest lace. Japanese gardens. Pebbled walks bordered by perfectly trimmed hedges. These are a sampling of the jewel-like scenes available for all to admire and emulate. A major advantage is that the raw materials are readily available and are often free.

Landscape architects, the professionals, often talk of scale, the relationship between the space and the items used to fill it. Certainly it is a difficult concept and one made particularly so because trees and shrubs often do not grow to our expectation. Nothing looks so stark as a handsome home with one or two full grown but scrawny trees, disappointing the homeowner. Trees grow at different rates and depend to a great extent on the soil and climate for their ultimate height and breadth. Therefore we have included in the final pages of this volume a map of the tree hardiness zones of America and Canada as a guide. It shows the prevalent temperature ranges throughout North America. There are photographs of houses silhouetted with in-scale illustrations of 24 commonly planted trees, showing those trees at the time of normal planting and at full growth.

There is a concise guide to flagging: how to lay stone as well as how to create the classic patterns. You will also find a chart depicting the special symbols used by landscape architects to help you read a professional blueprint or plan one of your own. There are construction details for paths and walkways including a cross-section of ground exposing the substructure.

For all the practical guidance offered at the end of this book, AROUND THE HOUSE is more than a how-to book. It is a work to be looked at often, each time concentrating on another aspect of landscaping. When the landscaper's efforts blend into the surroundings and nature takes over, making it impossible to determine what is and what was, then the landscaper receives the ultimate accolade. It is with this in mind that I took these pictures. I hope they prove meaningful, artful and enjoyable.

David Frazier
January 1979

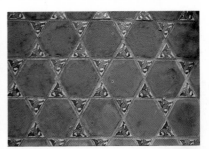

RELATIVE TREE SIZES

The size of trees and their rate of growth are governed in large part by climate and soil. Since these factors vary substantially even within the same hardiness zone, these tree illustrations are designed to suggest how the fullness and height of the full grown tree will appear in relation to the house.

The numbers below the tree names refer to the hardiness zone map.

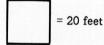 = 20 feet

10 years

50 years

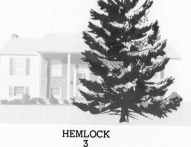

LINDEN
3, 4

LOMBARDY POPLAR
3

HEMLOCK
3

OLIVE
9

10 years

50 years

CALIFORNIA FAN PALM
8

SOUTHERN MAGNOLIA
7

WEEPING WILLOW
5, 6

MONTEREY PINE
7

10 years

50 years

EUROPEAN BEECH
4

EUROPEAN BIRCH
2

SUGAR MAPLE
3

RED MAPLE
3

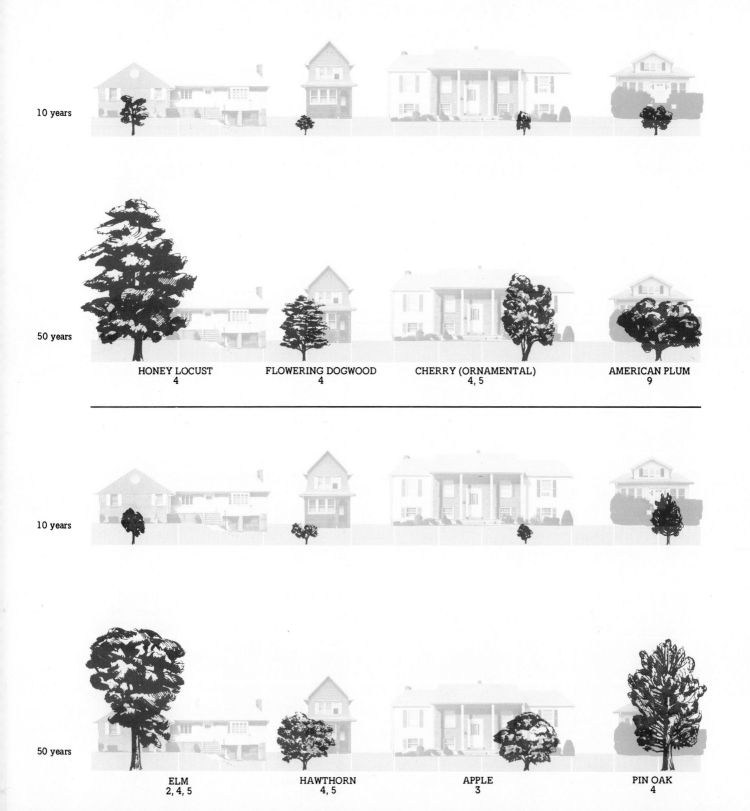

10 years

50 years

HONEY LOCUST
4

FLOWERING DOGWOOD
4

CHERRY (ORNAMENTAL)
4, 5

AMERICAN PLUM
9

10 years

50 years

ELM
2, 4, 5

HAWTHORN
4, 5

APPLE
3

PIN OAK
4

HARDINESS ZONES OF THE UNITED STATES AND CANADA

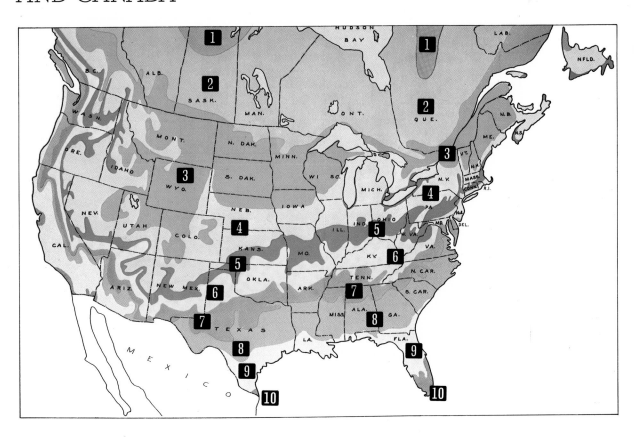

The limits of the average annual
minimum temperatures for each zone

Zone 1. Below -50° F.
2. -50° to -35°
3. -35° to -20°
4. -20° to -10°
5. -10° to -5°
6. -5° to 5°
7. 5° to 10°
8. 10° to 20°
9. 20° to 30°
10. 30° to 40°

Compiled by The Arnold Arboretum, Harvard University
Jamaica Plain, Mass.

FLAGGING PATTERNS

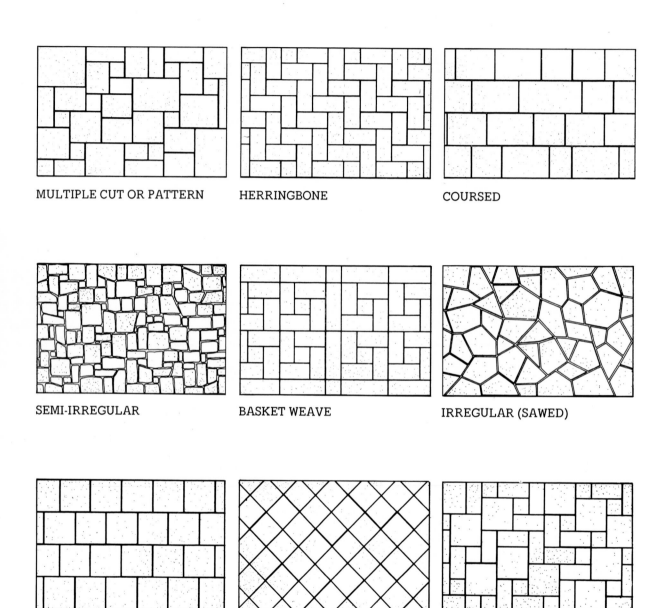

MULTIPLE CUT OR PATTERN

HERRINGBONE

COURSED

SEMI-IRREGULAR

BASKET WEAVE

IRREGULAR (SAWED)

ALL ONE SIZE

ALL ONE SIZE (DIAGONAL)

THREE SIZE PATTERN

FLAGGING CONSTRUCTION

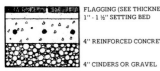
FLAGGING (SEE THICKNESS)
1" - 1 ½" SETTING BED

4" REINFORCED CONCRETE SLAB

4" CINDERS OR GRAVEL

FLAGGING (SEE THICKNESS)

4" SAND BED

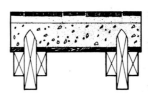
FLAGGING (SEE THICKNESS)
1" - 1½" SETTING

4" CONCRETE SLAB
WOOD SUB-FLOOR

WOOD BEAMS AND BRACING

ARCHITECTURAL SYMBOLS FOR LANDSCAPES

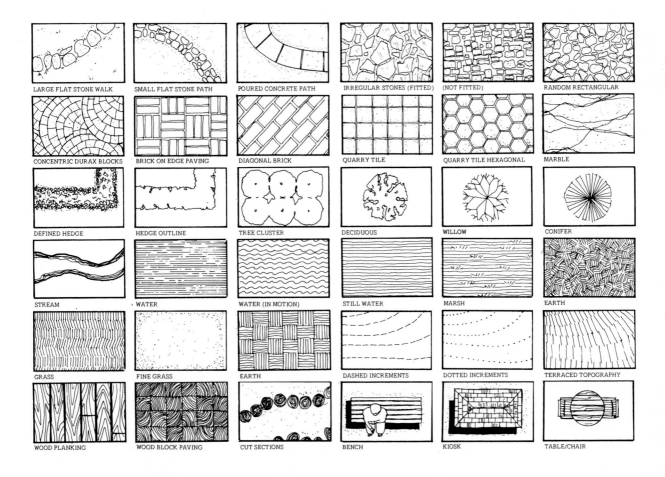

LARGE FLAT STONE WALK	SMALL FLAT STONE PATH	POURED CONCRETE PATH
IRREGULAR STONES (FITTED)	(NOT FITTED)	RANDOM RECTANGULAR
CONCENTRIC DURAX BLOCKS	BRICK ON EDGE PAVING	DIAGONAL BRICK
QUARRY TILE	QUARRY TILE HEXAGONAL	MARBLE
DEFINED HEDGE	HEDGE OUTLINE	TREE CLUSTER
DECIDUOUS	WILLOW	CONIFER
STREAM	WATER	WATER (IN MOTION)
STILL WATER	MARSH	EARTH
GRASS	FINE GRASS	EARTH
DASHED INCREMENTS	DOTTED INCREMENTS	TERRACED TOPOGRAPHY
WOOD PLANKING	WOOD BLOCK PAVING	CUT SECTIONS
BENCH	KIOSK	TABLE/CHAIR

ACKNOWLEDGMENTS

We appreciate the hospitality and generosity of all the people across the country who allowed us to photograph their homes and surroundings. Many thanks to you all for making this book possible.

Stuart Abercrombie
Bob Alfandre
Raymond Bahor
Burr Baker
Brian and Catherine Balkany
Marvin Banks
Mario Bisio
A. Alexander Blarek II, A.S.I.D.
Mr. and Mrs. William Blunt
Willis Harold Booth
Mr. and Mrs. Paul Bowman
Bill Brown
Mrs. June Carey
Caeser Castillo
Tim Choate
Bill Church
Mr. and Mrs. Lester Collins
Mrs. Miriam Crocker
Tober Delaney
Rogers A. Dockstader
Brian Donelly
Margot Patterson Doss
Paul Dwyer
Alfred Edelman
Jim Everett
Robert Flanders
Sid Galper
Michael Goldman
Abe Gordon
Charles Hansen
Miss Nancy Hay
Herb Hiller

Horst P. Horst
Edward Hume
Richard Jordan
Mr. and Mrs. John Kaufman
Andre Laport
Nicholas Lawford
Thomas L. Lockett
   (Land Images)
David Lynn
Doug Macey
Frank Mann
Bob Maybry
Zeb Mayhue
Harold A. Moldstad, Jr.
Daniel Mulhollan
Richard Painter
Mrs. Creighton Peet
Jack Post
Tom Prichard
Jack Prince
Richard Pryor
Joan Puma
Anne Reynolds
Don Roban
Jarvis Rockwell
Susan Merrill Rockwell
David Rust
Mrs. B.R. Sastanos
Max A. Schardt
G. James Scoggen
Sally Sesonske
Chris Spence

Lee Swerdlin
Mr. and Mrs. Buell Trowbridge
Susan Uhlman
Don Vallaster
Bruce Van Dyke
Doug Vernon
Mark Von Wald
Doris Walla
John Weller
Peter Chase Wilson
Torri Winkler
Jean W. Wolff
Sol Zaik